CITIZENS IN THE CROSSHAIRS: READY, AIM, HOLD YOUR FIRE?

Shortly before 10 o'clock on the morning of September 30, 2011, a group of men including an al Qaeda leader finished eating breakfast and headed toward their vehicles near the remote town of Khashef in Yemen's northern Al Jawf province. Unbeknownst to them, the men had been under constant surveillance for some time. Overhead, two armed Predator unmanned aerial systems (UAS)—commonly referred to as drones— closed in on the group. Operated by the Central Intelligence Agency (CIA), the Predators fired Hellfire missiles killing the men, including the al Qaeda leader.[1]

On its face, the above scenario would seem fairly unremarkable to most observers. In over 10 years of prosecuting its war on terror, the United States has conducted hundreds of similar strikes. In fact, however, the scenario is quite remarkable for one simple fact: the al Qaeda leader intentionally targeted and killed that day, Anwar al-Awlaki, was a U.S. citizen.[2]

Since September 11, 2001, the United States has pursued a largely military approach to fighting terrorism abroad. This approach is anchored domestically in the Authorization for Use of Military Force (AUMF), a joint resolution passed by Congress on September 18, 2001, which authorizes the President to

> use all necessary and appropriate force against those nations, organizations, or persons he determines planned, authorized, committed, or aided the terrorist attacks that occurred on September 11, 2001, or harbored such organizations or persons, in order to prevent any future acts of international terrorism against the United States by such nations, organizations or persons.[3]

In its use of "necessary and appropriate force," the executive branch has increasingly employed the tactic of targeted killing, typically through armed UAS strikes conducted by the Department of Defense (DoD) and the CIA, or kill or capture missions directed by the Joint Special Operations Command (JSOC), such as the Navy SEAL raid that killed Osama bin Laden.[4] While the latter constitute the majority of targeted killing operations, the use of armed UAS strikes has steadily grown as a cheaper, safer, and arguably more precise alternative to boots on the ground.[5]

Despite its increased use, targeted killing has proved divisive, generating considerable controversy on legal and moral grounds.[6] Domestically, the debate surrounding the practice rose to a crescendo first following the disclosure in January 2010 of al-Awlaki's inclusion on DoD and CIA kill or capture lists, and again when he was successfully targeted and killed.[7] Critics variously claim that targeted killing is contrary to international and human rights law, and that the U.S. government's lethal targeting of its own citizens violates domestic law. Moreover, supporters and critics alike express dismay over the government's lack of transparency and perceived lack of accountability.

This paper first defines targeted killing, then frames the debate over the lethal targeting of U.S. citizens. Next, the paper demonstrates that under the right circumstances, the U.S. government may—as the Obama Administration asserts—lawfully pursue a policy of lethally targeting its citizens abroad. Finally, the paper argues that while there is currently broad domestic support for the lethal targeting of suspected terrorists overseas—including those who happen to be U.S. citizens—the continued viability of such a policy relies in no small measure on increased transparency and accountability.[8]

Defining Targeted Killing

There is no universally accepted definition of targeted killing. Indeed, the term became commonplace only in 2000 when Israel openly acknowledged an official policy of targeted killing in response to the second intifada.[9] In a case challenging that policy, the Israeli Supreme Court characterized the practice as security forces acting "to kill members of terrorist organizations involved in the planning, launching, or execution of terrorist attacks against Israel."[10] Some commentators define the term broadly to encompass a state's intentional use of lethal force in a wide range of contexts from armed conflict, to assassination, to law enforcement.[11] Others define it more narrowly, strictly limiting the practice to armed conflict.[12]

This paper addresses the employment of targeted killing in the context of the U.S. war on terror, which includes not only armed conflict but also the use of force in self-defense that may not rise to the level of armed conflict. Accordingly, the paper defines targeted killing as a state's intentional killing of a specific individual who is an unlawful combatant, during armed conflict or the legitimate exercise of national self-defense.

The adjective "unlawful" is significant. The law of war recognizes two categories of individuals in international (i.e., state versus state) armed conflict: combatants and civilians.[13] Combatants include members of the armed forces of a state that is a party to an armed conflict, and everyone else who satisfies the criteria for prisoner of war status.[14] Importantly, combatants have "the right to participate directly in hostilities," and may be targeted anywhere, at any time, so long as they are not *hors de combat*.[15] Everyone else is a civilian.[16] Civilians may not be intentionally targeted but have an obligation not to directly participate in hostilities. Civilians who disregard that obligation become "unlawful combatants" and lose their immunity from attack, at least for the period of direct participation.[17]

3

The law of war does not expressly recognize a combatant category in non-international (i.e., state versus non-state actor) armed conflict. Non-state actors have no legal right to participate in hostilities and, as in international armed conflict, civilians lose their immunity from targeting when they directly participate in hostilities.[18] For purposes of this paper, therefore, non-state actors and civilians directly participating in hostilities during non-international armed conflict are considered "unlawful combatants."

The Debate Over Targeted Killing

Scholars and commentators have debated the legality of U.S. targeted killing practices from the outset. Fundamentally, much of the debate revolves around the broader question of whether to address terrorism as a military or law enforcement issue. Some critics allege, for example, that targeted killings are essentially assassinations or extra-judicial executions violative of human rights law.[19] Others claim that while targeted killing may be lawful within the scope of armed conflict, U.S. practice impermissibly goes beyond that scope, potentially violating the sovereignty of other states.[20] Moreover, critics express concern that targeted killings have impacted a disproportionate number of civilians.[21] Proponents of targeted killing counter that it is distinguishable from assassination; that while state sovereignty is an important consideration, the U.S. should not be tied to a single "hot" battlefield while Al Qaeda and Associated Movements (AQAM) are able to relocate their operations at will; and that while civilian casualties are regrettable and mistakes sometimes occur, targeted killing is overall a very precise tool.

The disclosure of Anwar al-Awlaki's addition to DoD and CIA kill or capture lists propelled the debate into the forefront of domestic discourse with a newly narrowed focus: the legality of lethally targeting U.S. citizens.[22] In August 2010, two civil rights groups, the American Civil Liberties Union (ACLU) and the Center for Constitutional Rights (CCR), filed a lawsuit in federal court on behalf of al-Awlaki's father, Nasser al-Awlaki. Among other relief, the suit asked the court to order the government to "disclose the criteria that are used in determining whether the government will carry out the targeted killing of a U.S. citizen."[23] While dismissing the suit on procedural grounds, the presiding judge remarked that "[s]tark, and perplexing, questions readily come to mind," but "the serious issues regarding the merits of the alleged authorization of the targeted killing of a U.S. citizen overseas must await another day or another (non-judicial) forum."[24] Although the lawsuit failed to shed light on the government's justification for lethally targeting U.S. citizens, al-Awlaki's death would have the opposite effect.

The day of the strike that killed al-Awlaki, the *Washington Post* reported the existence of a secret Justice Department legal opinion, drafted in 2010 by the Office of Legal Counsel (OLC), addressing whether al-Awlaki could be lawfully targeted.[25] Though the administration declined to comment officially, within days "people who [had] read the document" leaked details to the press.[26] According to the *New York Times*, the opinion's authors considered both international and domestic law, including the law of war, state sovereignty, an executive order banning assassination, a criminal statute applicable to the murder of citizens abroad by other U.S. citizens, and constitutional protections like the Fifth Amendment's Due Process Clause.[27] The OLC opinion reportedly concluded that al-Awlaki, identified by intelligence agencies as an operational leader for Al Qaeda in the Arabian Peninsula (AQAP)—an organization with ties to al Qaeda—fell under the scope of the 2001 AUMF; that he posed an imminent threat to the United States; and that he could be lawfully targeted without violating international or domestic law if his capture were not feasible.[28]

Al-Awlaki's death provoked strong responses from both ends of the political spectrum.[29] Criticism initially focused on the lack of due process afforded a U.S. citizen, but quickly grew to include the lack of government transparency. A growing chorus of both critics and supporters of the government's action, including legal scholars, commentators, media organizations, and politicians, has repeatedly called on the Obama Administration to release the OLC opinion or some variation thereof.[30]

Likely in response to the criticism, DoD General Counsel Jeh Johnson and Attorney General Eric Holder finally addressed some of these issues in recent speeches, the latter providing the administration's most detailed legal justification to date for lethally targeting U.S. citizens as part of the war on terror.[31] Many observers found Holder's comments sorely wanting, however, and little more than confirmation of what had already been leaked to the press.[32]

Notably, however, Holder summarized the administration's position as to when the government can lethally target a U.S. citizen. According to Holder, when acting in compliance with the principles of the law of war, the targeted killing of a U.S. citizen is permissible *at least* when that citizen:

- is located in a foreign country,
- is a senior operational leader of AQAM,
- is "actively engaged in planning to kill Americans,"
- "poses an imminent threat of violent attack against the United States," and
- cannot feasibly be captured.[33]

Moreover, Holder provided insight into the administration's stance on due process in this context. He conceded the relevance of constitutional considerations, noting the U.S. Supreme Court's balancing test approach to the Fifth Amendment's Due Process Clause weighing the private and government interests involved, as well as the burdens the government might face in providing additional process. To emphasize the significance of both the government's interest and the burdens it might face in this particular context, Holder asserted that, "Where national security operations are at stake, due process takes into account the realities of combat."[34]

Rejecting calls for *ex ante* judicial review of executive branch decisions to lethally target U.S. citizens, Holder noted that, "'Due process' and 'judicial process' are not one and the same, particularly when it comes to national security."[35] In support of that assertion, he observed that courts have historically recognized national security operations, such as targeting, as "core functions" of the executive branch.[36] Without articulating the Obama Administration's standard for what process is due when lethally targeting U.S. citizens, Holder asserted that such operations have "robust oversight" and that the administration "regularly informs the appropriate members of Congress about counterterrorism activities."[37]

International Law Bases for Targeted Killing

Echoing earlier statements by State Department Legal Advisor Harold Hongju Koh and Assistant to the President for Homeland Security and Counterterrorism John Brennan, in his speech Attorney General Holder justified targeted killing under the paradigms of armed conflict and national self-defense.[38]

Regulated by the law of war, the context of armed conflict affords states the greatest latitude for the employment of force, including targeted killing. The law of war provides that combatants may target not only other combatants, but sometimes even civilians who would normally be immune from deliberate attack. Under a traditional view, because they are technically civilians, members of non-state actors like AQAM may be intentionally targeted only while directly participating in hostilities (e.g., while attacking combatants). This approach has led to a frustrating "revolving door" phenomenon—the proverbial farmer by day, fighter by night—that many believe provides an inordinate amount of civilian protection to individuals who arguably do not deserve it.

After some six years of expert discussions addressing this and other concerns, in 2009 the International Committee of the Red Cross (ICRC) published interpretive guidance on the concept of direct participation in hostilities. According to the guidance, "members of organized armed groups belonging to a non-State party to an armed conflict cease to be civilians" and lose their immunity from direct attack for the duration of their membership if engaged in a "continuous combat function."[39] Continuous combat function includes "the preparation, execution, or command of acts or operations amounting to direct participation in hostilities."[40] Some argue that the ICRC interpretive guidance does not go far enough in solving the revolving door issue.[41] Nonetheless, the combination of the traditional "direct participation in hostilities" standard for the occasional "foot soldier," and the "continuous combatant function" standard for those whose role is more significant, provides substantial leeway to lethally target members of armed groups like AQAM.

Some claim that the United States has cast the armed conflict net too wide, however. These critics assert that while the United States maintains it is engaged in a "global" conflict with AQAM, it is presently engaged in only a single armed conflict to which the law of war and its more permissive targeting rules apply: the non-international

8

armed conflict in Afghanistan.[42] Hence, they argue, targeted killings that occur outside

Afghanistan—in places like Pakistan and Yemen—cannot be justified under the law of

war. According to press reports, this very debate is taking place within the Obama

Administration.[43] Attorney General Holder and other senior administration officials,

however, publicly advocate the expansive view.[44]

Regardless, as Holder asserted, the United States also relies on the right of

national self-defense—initially triggered by the September 11 attacks, well established

in customary international law, and explicitly recognized in Article 51 of the UN

Charter—as an alternative justification for targeted killing.[45] Some hold that the right of

self-defense applies only in the case of an actual armed attack. The United States,

however, has long viewed self-defense to apply also against an imminent use of force

(i.e., anticipatory self-defense) or a continuing threat.[46] Given continued and threatened

attacks by AQAM against the United States and its interests around the world, it is

therefore reasonable for the United States to assert a right to exercise self-defense

under this theory without being geographically limited to states where a *de jure* armed

conflict exists. The opposite conclusion would effectively create safe havens from which

AQAM could plan and launch attacks against United States interests with relative

impunity.[47]

The most significant limiting factor under this expansive view of self-defense is

the principle of state sovereignty, itself enshrined in the UN Charter. Article 2(4) of the

Charter provides that, "All Members shall refrain in their international relations from the

threat or use of force against the territorial integrity or political independence of any

state . . . ."[48] The Obama Administration is clearly sensitive to this issue. After asserting

9

that U.S. legal authority is not limited to Afghanistan, Holder conceded that, "This does not mean that we can use military force whenever or wherever we want. International legal principles, including respect for another nation's sovereignty, constrain our ability to act unilaterally."[49]

Holder also argued that sovereignty issues are not entirely insurmountable, however. He noted that a state whose sovereignty is at issue can simply consent to intervention. While domestic concerns may preclude their public acknowledgment, both Yemen and Pakistan reportedly consented to U.S. use of force—including targeted killing—against AQAM targets within their borders.[50] Moreover, Holder asserted that a state that is unwilling or unable to suppress a threat coming from within its borders cannot claim sovereignty to shield itself from the legitimate use of self-defense by another state harmed by the threat. Throughout its history, the United States has repeatedly exercised its right to self-defense on this basis.[51] In fact, such a scenario led to the 2001 United States invasion of Afghanistan after the Taliban rejected President Bush's ultimatum to surrender all al Qaeda leaders present in Afghanistan, and immediately and permanently close all terrorist training camps located there.[52]

Targeting U.S. Citizens

In 2009 or early 2010, U.S. targeted killing policy underwent a significant change: for the first time, a U.S. citizen—Anwar al-Awlaki—was added to the DoD and CIA kill or capture lists.[53] Al-Awlaki was a Yemeni-American dual citizen who, according to the U.S. government, became an operational leader for AQAP and had ties to both the alleged "Fort Hood shooter," MAJ Nidal Hasan, and the so-called "Underwear Bomber," Umar Farouk Abdulmutallab.[54] A September 30, 2011 CIA Predator strike in Yemen killed al-Awlaki and, coincidentally, another U.S. citizen named Samir Khan, the co-editor of an English-language al Qaeda web magazine. Khan was not a target of the strike.

Domestically, both reports in January 2010 of al-Awlaki's selection for targeted killing and the subsequent news of his death sparked intense debate over the propriety of a U.S. president ordering the "execution without trial" of a U.S. citizen. While U.S. targeted killing practices appear justifiable under international law, is the same true under domestic law when the target is a U.S. citizen?

Fifth Amendment

"No person shall be . . . deprived of life . . . without due process of law . . . ."[55] Civil liberties groups, commentators, politicians—and, interestingly, even AQAP—have denounced al-Awlaki's targeted killing as violative of the Fifth Amendment's due process guarantees.[56] Historical practice and U.S. Supreme Court jurisprudence, however, demonstrate that even U.S. citizens are subject to the law of war during armed conflict. The ACLU and CCR appear to concede this point as their lawsuit alleged that, absent certain circumstances, the targeted killing of U.S. citizens violates the Fifth Amendment "*outside of armed conflict.*"[57] The U.S. Civil War experience bears this out.

Throughout the course of the Civil War, Congress never declared war on the Confederacy. Nor did President Lincoln officially recognize the Confederacy as a belligerent, fearing that doing so would confer legitimacy on its claim of independence. He instead viewed secession as an invalid act with no legal effect, such that Confederates remained U.S. citizens.[58] Faced with an armed rebellion by U.S. citizens, the government adopted a novel legal approach giving rebels a "double character": they were at the same time criminals, subject to criminal prosecution with concomitant

11

constitutional protections, and enemies, subject solely to the law of war.[59] The government had discretion to choose which paradigm to apply.

The Supreme Court sustained this "double character" approach in *The Prize Cases*, involving the seizure of four vessels violating President Lincoln's 1861 blockade of southern ports. The ships' owners maintained that the United States did not have the right to seize their cargoes as "enemies' property" because "the term 'enemy' is properly applicable to those only who are subjects or citizens of a foreign State at war with our own."[60] Moreover, the owners asserted that they had a "right to claim the protection of the government for their persons and property, and to be treated as loyal citizens till legally convicted of having renounced their allegiance and made war against the Government . . . ."[61] Rejecting those arguments, the Court observed that, "it is a proposition never doubted that the belligerent party who claims to be sovereign may exercise both the belligerent and sovereign rights."[62] The Court then declared that the owners "have cast off their allegiance and made war on their Government, and are nonetheless enemies because they are traitors."[63]

Subsequent Supreme Court decisions continue to find that U.S. citizens can be enemy belligerents subject to the law of war. In *Ex Parte Quirin*, a World War II case, eight German saboteurs—including Herbert Hans Haupt, a U.S. citizen—sought a writ of habeas corpus after being tried and sentenced to death by a military tribunal.[64] The saboteurs alleged that President Roosevelt had no authority to try them by military tribunal, and that they were instead entitled to criminal trials in civil court with Fifth and Sixth Amendment protections. A unanimous Court rejected the saboteurs' arguments and, with respect to Haupt, remarked that, "Citizenship in the United States of an enemy belligerent does not relieve him from the consequences of a belligerency which is unlawful because in violation of the law of war."[65]

A more recent Supreme Court case, *Hamdi v. Rumsfeld*, quoted *Ex Parte Quirin* approvingly, adding that, "A citizen, no less than an alien, can be 'part of or supporting forces hostile to the United States or coalition partners' and 'engaged in an armed conflict against the United States.'"[66] Nonetheless, in a plurality opinion the Court established that a U.S. citizen captured and held as an enemy combatant was entitled to *some* due process. Born in Louisiana, Yaser Esam Hamdi moved to Saudi Arabia as a child before being captured by the Northern Alliance in Afghanistan in 2001 and turned over to the United States.[67] After detaining him at Guantanamo Bay, Cuba, the government transferred Hamdi to military brigs in Virginia and South Carolina upon learning of his U.S. citizenship. Hamdi disputed his designation as an "enemy combatant" who could be detained until the cessation of hostilities. The U.S. Court of Appeals for the Fourth Circuit held that Hamdi's detention was lawful and that he was not entitled to an opportunity to challenge his enemy combatant designation.

To assess whether Hamdi had been afforded sufficient procedural due process, the plurality applied the standard it established in a 1976 case involving the termination of Social Security benefits, *Mathews v. Eldridge*. *Mathews* requires balancing the individual's interests that the official action will affect against the government's interests, including the burdens greater due process would impose on the government.[68] Finding that Hamdi's liberty interest outweighed the government's interest in detaining him as an enemy combatant, the Court vacated the Fourth Circuit's decision, holding that due process required that Hamdi "receive notice of the factual basis for his classification, and a fair opportunity to rebut the government's factual assertions before a neutral decisionmaker."[69]

Applying the result in *Hamdi*, some argue that if a U.S. citizen *detained* by the government is entitled to due process, surely a U.S. citizen is also entitled to at least as much due process before the government can intentionally target and *kill* him. While that proposition sounds reasonable on its face, it ignores important factual distinctions. *Hamdi* applies to a citizen challenging the basis for his detention who is already in the hands of the government and being held in the United States. Indeed, the plurality noted that,

> The parties agree that initial captures on the battlefield need not receive the process we have discussed here; that process is due only when the determination is made to *continue* to hold those who have been seized.[70]

This language reflects a desire to avoid unduly interfering with the executive branch's prosecution of an armed conflict and suggests a distinction between pre- and post-capture situations. Once captured, an enemy poses little continuing risk to the United States and, therefore, should plausibly be entitled to exercise at least some of the constitutional rights he is otherwise entitled to.[71] On the other hand, an enemy at large represents an ongoing threat. While a seductive argument, *Hamdi* cannot therefore be read as requiring notice and an opportunity to be heard prior to the targeted killing of a U.S. citizen. Rather, some suggest, *Hamdi* seems to require only the possibility of *ex post* judicial review.[72] Moreover, the executive branch can arguably meet its due process obligations through robust internal and perhaps external oversight mechanisms, as discussed below.

14

<u>Assassination Ban</u>

Attorney General Holder distinguished targeted killing from assassination, characterizing the latter as "unlawful killings" while justifying the former under the law of war.[73] Others disagree, however, contending that the targeted killing of a U.S. citizen like al-Awlaki violates Executive Order (E.O.) 12333's ban on assassinations.[74] Issued by President Reagan in 1981, this executive order carries forward an assassination ban first promulgated by President Ford in 1976, in response to a Senate select committee's report addressing allegations of United States involvement in assassination plots against foreign political leaders.[75] While E.O. 12333 does not define "assassination," a 1989 memorandum on the assassination ban written by W. Hays Parks, then the Special Assistant for Law of War Matters to The Judge Advocate General of the Army, is considered fairly authoritative. According to Parks, "assassination involves murder of a targeted individual for political purposes."[76] He concluded that E.O. 12333 does not preclude the use of military force against "legitimate targets" during both armed conflict and peacetime (i.e., during the exercise of self-defense).[77]

Parks addressed only the use of force by members of the armed forces, however, who are considered combatants and therefore entitled under the law of war to combatant immunity for their warlike acts.[78] Some commentators observe that while the assassination ban does not apply to armed forces personnel, the same may not be true for targeted killings carried out by CIA personnel.[79] This issue may well be moot because of secret counterterrorism authorities granted to the CIA by Presidents Reagan, Clinton, and George W. Bush, reportedly including at least limited sanction of overseas assassinations.[80] Moreover, even if targeted killing as a U.S. counterterrorism tactic were deemed subject to E.O. 12333, the President could simply modify or even revoke the executive order.

Foreign Murder Statute

Title 18, section 1119(b) of the U.S. Code—commonly referred to as the foreign murder statute—makes it a crime for "[a] person who, being a national of the U.S., kills or attempts to kill a national of the U.S. while such national is outside the U.S. but within the jurisdiction of another country."[81] Some assert that this statute precludes the targeted killing of U.S. citizens, at least when carried out by someone other than a "lawful" combatant.[82]

Long ago, the U.S. Supreme Court decided that "an act of Congress ought never to be construed to violate the law of nations, if any other possible construction remains."[83] Applying this rule of construction, the law of war—which, as discussed above, permits the targeting of combatants, whether lawful or not, during armed conflict or in the exercise of self-defense—displaces the domestic law of the foreign murder statute. Accordingly, the foreign murder statute would not make the targeted killing of a U.S. citizen a criminal act in the context of an armed conflict or self-defense.[84]

As with E.O. 12333's assassination ban, this conclusion may depend on the status of the individual who actually "pulls the trigger": while a member of the armed forces entitled to combatant immunity would not be subject to the foreign murder statute, someone like a CIA employee arguably would.[85] Once again, however, authorities granted to the CIA could render the issue moot. Moreover, the foreign murder statute provides that, "[n]o prosecution may be instituted against any person under this section except upon the written approval of the Attorney General, the Deputy Attorney General, or an Assistant Attorney General . . . ."[86] It seems inconceivable that,

16

having ordered a CIA employee to engage in targeted killing, an administration would authorize the employee's subsequent prosecution under the foreign murder statute. Absent a presidential pardon, however, a subsequent administration would not be precluded from undertaking such a prosecution.[87]

In sum, while lingering concerns exist, the Obama Administration appears justified in its assertion that international and domestic law permit the targeted killing of U.S. citizens.

Transparency and Accountability

On his first day in office, President Obama told the White House senior staff that, "The way to make Government responsible is to hold it accountable. And the way to make Government accountable is to make it transparent so that the American people can know exactly what decisions are being made, how they're being made, and whether their interests are being well served."[88]

So far, there has been little transparency and no public accountability regarding the executive branch's use of targeted killing. While some degree of secrecy is understandable—perhaps even a substantial degree, at least with respect to information that might compromise intelligence sources and methods—the government must be more forthcoming with the American people if it wants to maintain the viability of this increasingly important tactic in the war on terror, especially where the targeting of U.S. citizens is involved.

Transparency

Until recent comments by President Obama and a few senior administration officials, the government did not even publicly acknowledge its practice of targeted killing outside Iraq and Afghanistan, much less the lethal targeting of a U.S. citizen.[89]

17

The majority of information about the practice comes from media reports citing anonymous sources. Indeed, when the ACLU submitted Freedom of Information Act (FOIA) requests to the CIA and OLC seeking records pertaining to al-Awlaki's targeted killing, both responded that they could "neither confirm nor deny" the existence of the types of documents requested.[90] After receiving a similar response from OLC, the *New York Times* filed a lawsuit against the Department of Justice seeking compelled disclosure.[91]

Good reasons exist for remaining tight-lipped about targeted killing operations. It goes without saying that certain information cannot be released as it could jeopardize classified sources and methods, or the accomplishment of particular operations. There may also be diplomatic reasons that militate against disclosure. For instance, some of the states where those operations occur, such as Pakistan and Yemen, are reticent to acknowledge their cooperation in domestically unpopular UAS strikes; public statements by the U.S. government would not help matters. Nonetheless, targeted killing operations are among the government's worst kept secrets—not only because their effects are very public, but also because of the significant number of media leaks attributed to government officials. As one observer quipped, "Either this program is a secret, in which case the government should stop talking to Charlie [Savage of the *New York Times*] about it, or it's not a secret, in which case it should figure out what is releasable in the [OLC] memo and release it."[92]

As demonstrated above, one can make a good faith legal argument in support of the targeted killing of U.S. citizens. Nevertheless, prominent legal scholars dispute the practice's legality.[93] Similarly, unlike the overwhelmingly positive domestic reaction to

Osama bin Laden's death during a kill or capture mission, the reaction to al-Awlaki's targeted killing has prompted mixed reactions from politicians, pundits, and the American public alike.[94] The subject is sufficiently sensitive, controversial, and significant—it is, after all, the government's exercise of the power to take a life, seemingly with little or no constraint—that the executive branch should do all it can to convince doubters of the validity of its actions.

The Obama Administration is laudably moving toward greater transparency with recent speeches by DoD General Counsel Johnson and especially Attorney General Holder that at least outline the administration's legal reasoning. Speeches are insufficient, however. The next logical step is to release the OLC opinion itself, or some form thereof. Jack Goldsmith, a former assistant attorney general who oversaw OLC from 2003-2004, posits that the legal analysis "can be disclosed without revealing means or methods of intelligence-gathering or jeopardizing technical covertness."[95] Doing so, he argues, "would permit a robust debate about targeted killings – especially of U.S. citizens – that is troubling to many people," and, in the end, would likely "show the Obama administration in a very good light to most American audiences."[96]

Accountability

Like transparency, U.S. targeted killing practices lack public accountability. Little is known about the process for adding U.S. citizens to kill or capture lists. According to Secretary of Defense Leon Panetta, DoD and the CIA nominate individuals for inclusion on those lists, and the President makes the final decision.[97] Important questions remain, however. What evidentiary standards are applied? Who confirms the intelligence used to vet targets, and how? How are targets positively identified to mitigate the risk of error? Who determines that a target cannot be captured and must instead be killed, and how? What checks and balances exist?

Most troubling, perhaps, is the lack of independent review of decisions to lethally target U.S. citizens. While the Constitution vests the President with substantial national security powers, those powers are not absolute. A President's seemingly unfettered discretion in secretly determining whether U.S. citizens should be killed does little to reassure a leery public and instead creates the appearance of a veritable star chamber. According to Attorney General Holder, the executive branch neither has, nor should ever have, "the ability to target [U.S. citizens] without robust oversight."[98] The only evidence of oversight he offers, however, is the administration's briefing "appropriate members of Congress about our counterterrorism activities, including the legal framework."[99] Those members apparently do not include Senator Patrick Leahy, chairman of the Senate Judiciary Committee, who told Holder just days after Holder's speech that he "still [wanted] to see the Office of Legal Counsel memorandum."[100] This suggests that current oversight is insufficient.

Additional oversight could come in various forms, both within and outside the executive branch, and may satisfy due process requirements. One option would be to follow the lead of the Israeli Supreme Court. In its review of Israeli targeted killing practices, that court required the implementation of measures intended to mitigate the risk of erroneous targeting and abuses, including an independent and thorough investigation after each targeted killing operation "regarding the precision of the identification of the target and the circumstances of the attack upon him."[101] Some suggest the establishment of an independent office within the executive branch to

20

conduct such investigations, perhaps along the lines of the CIA's independent inspector general.[102]

Alternatively, targeted killing decisions could be subjected to judicial review.[103] Attorney General Holder rejected *ex ante* judicial review out of hand, citing the Constitution's allocation of national security operations to the executive branch and the need for timely action.[104] Courts are indeed reluctant to stray into the realm of political questions, as evidenced by the district court's dismissal of the ACLU and CCR lawsuit. On the other hand, a model for a special court that operates in secret already exists: the Foreign Intelligence Surveillance Court (FISC) that oversees requests for surveillance warrants for suspected foreign agents. While *ex ante* judicial review would provide the most robust form of oversight, *ex post* review by a court like the FISC would nonetheless serve as a significant check on executive power.[105]

Regardless of the type of oversight implemented, some form of independent review is necessary to demonstrate accountability and bolster confidence in the targeted killing process.

Conclusion

The United States has increasingly relied on targeted killing as an important tactic in its war on terror and will continue to do so for the foreseeable future.[106] This is entirely reasonable given current budgetary constraints and the appeal of targeted killing, especially UAS strikes, as an alternative to the use of conventional forces. Moreover, the United States will likely again seek to employ the tactic against U.S. citizens assessed to be operational leaders of AQAM. As demonstrated above, one can make a good faith argument that doing so is entirely permissible under both international and domestic law as the Obama Administration claims, the opinions of

21

some prominent legal scholars notwithstanding. The viability of future lethal targeting of

U.S. citizens is questionable, however, if the government fails to address legitimate

issues of transparency and accountability. While the administration has recently made

progress on the transparency front, much more remains to be done, including the

release in some form of the legal analysis contained in OLC's 2010 opinion. Moreover,

the administration must be able to articulate to the American people how it selects U.S.

citizens for targeted killing and the safeguards in place to mitigate the risk of error and

abuse. Finally, these targeting decisions must be subject to some form of independent

review that will both satisfy due process and boost public confidence.

Endnotes

[1] See, for example, Sudarsan Raghavan, "Anwar Al-Aulaqi, US born cleric linked to al Qaeda killed Yemen says," *Washington Post*, September 30, 2011. Media reports are somewhat inconsistent regarding the details of al-Awlaki's death, some reporting that the strikes killed al-Awlaki and his companions as they headed to their vehicles after breakfast, others reporting that he was riding in a convoy at the time. The reports relied on statements from unnamed United States officials, Yemeni officials, and local citizens. Until Secretary of Defense Leon Panetta's recent *60 Minutes* interview, the United States did not publicly acknowledge responsibility for the operation. Leon Panetta, "The Defense Secretary: Leon Panetta," interview by Scott Pelley, *60 Minutes*, CBS, January 29, 2012, http://www.cbsnews.com/8301-18560_162-57367997/the-defense-secretary-an-interview-with-leon-panetta/?tag=currentVideoInfo;videoMetaInfo (accessed February 22, 2012).

[2] Al-Awlaki is also spelled al-Aulaqi.

[3] Authorization for Use of Military Force, Pub. L. 107-40, 115 Stat. 224 (2001), sec. 2(a).

[4] Dana Priest and William M. Arkin, "'Top Secret America': A look at the military's Joint Special Operations Command," *Washington Post*, September 2, 2011. See also *Frontline*, "Kill/Capture," Public Broadcasting Service, May 10, 2011, transcript, http://www.pbs.org/wgbh/pages/frontline/afghanistan-pakistan/kill-capture/transcript/ (accessed January 20, 2012).

[5] Scott Shane and Thom Shanker, "Strike Reflects U.S. Shift to Drones in Terror Fight," *New York Times*, October 1, 2011; Greg Miller and Julie Tate, "CIA shifts focus to killing targets," *Washington Post*, September 2, 2011. For statistics reflecting the growing use of UAS strikes, see New America Foundation, *The Year of the Drone: An Analysis of U.S. Drone Strikes*

in Pakistan, 2004-2012, http://counterterrorism.newamerica.net/drones#2011chart (accessed February 29, 2012).

[6] For a discussion of the moral dimension of targeted killing, which is beyond the scope of this paper, see, for example, Peter M. Cullen, "The Role of Targeted Killing in the Campaign Against Terror," *Joint Force Quarterly* 48 (1st quarter 2008): 22.

[7] Dana Priest, "U.S. military teams, intelligence deeply involved in aiding Yemen on strikes," *Washington Post*, January 27, 2010. See also Scott Shane, "U.S. Approves Targeted Killing of American Cleric," *New York Times*, April 6, 2010.

[8] According to a Washington Post-ABC News Poll of a random national sample of 1,000 adults conducted February 1-4, 2012, 83 percent of those polled approved of "[t]he use of unmanned, 'drone' aircraft against terrorist suspects overseas," and 65 percent approved even "if those suspected terrorists are American citizens living in other countries." *Washington Post*, "Washington Post-ABC News Poll," *PostPolitics*, http://www.washingtonpost.com/wp-srv/politics/polls/postabcpoll_020412.html (accessed March 15, 2012).

[9] Laura Blumenfeld, "In Israel, a Divisive Struggle Over Targeted Killing," *Washington Post*, August 27, 2006; UN General Assembly, Human Rights Council, 14th Session, *Report of the Special Rapporteur on extrajudicial, summary or arbitrary executions, Philip Alston. Addendum: Study on targeted killings*, A/HRC/14/24/Add.6, May 28, 2010 (hereinafter Alston Report), 4.

[10] The Public Committee Against Torture v. Israel, HCJ 769/02, para. 2 (2005), http://elyon1.court.gov.il/Files_ENG/02/690/007/a34/02007690.a34.pdf (accessed November 20, 2011).

[11] For example a United Nations report defined targeted killing as "the intentional, premeditated and deliberate use of lethal force, by States or their agents acting under colour of law, or by an organized armed group in armed conflict, against a specific individual who is not in the physical custody of the perpetrator." Alston Report, 3.

[12] Professor Gary Solis, for example, defines targeted killing as,

> [T]he intentional killing of a specific civilian or unlawful combatant who cannot reasonably be apprehended, who is taking a direct part in hostilities, the targeting done at the direction of the state, in the context of an international or non-international armed conflict.

Gary D. Solis, *The Law of Armed Conflict: International Humanitarian Law in War* (New York: Cambridge University Press, 2010), 538.

[13] The law of war (LOW) is also referred to as the law of armed conflict (LOAC) and international humanitarian law (IHL).

[14] Geneva Convention Relative to the Treatment of Prisoners of War, August 12, 1949, 6 U.S.T. 3316, 75 U.N.T.S. 135, art. 4. The criteria for prisoner of war status include: being commanded by a person responsible for his subordinates; having a fixed, distinctive sign recognizable at a distance; carrying arms openly; and, conducting their operations in accordance with the laws and customs of war. Ibid. A 1977 treaty supplementing the 1949

Geneva Conventions, Additional Protocol I, dropped the requirement for wearing a fixed, distinctive sign. Protocol Additional to the Geneva Conventions of 12 August 1949, and Relating to the Protection of Victims of International Armed Conflicts (Protocol I), June 8, 1977 (hereinafter Additional Protocol I), art. 44(3). For this reason and others, the U.S. has chosen not to ratify Additional Protocol I though it considers many of the treaty's other provisions to reflect binding customary international law.

[15] Additional Protocol I, art. 43(2); A combatant is *hors de combat* if he "is in the power of an adverse Party" (typically as a prisoner of war), "clearly expresses an intent to surrender," or is incapable of defending himself as a result of wounds, sickness, or unconsciousness. Ibid., art. 41.

[16] Ibid., art. 50.

[17] Ibid., art. 51(3).

[18] International Committee of the Red Cross, "The relevance of IHL in the context of terrorism," January 1, 2011, http://www.icrc.org/eng/resources/documents/misc/terrorism-ihl-210705.htm (accessed February 25, 2012); Protocol Additional to the Geneva Conventions of 12 August 1949, and Relating to the Protection of Victims of Non-International Armed Conflicts (Protocol II), June 8, 1977, art. 13. As with Additional Protocol I, the U.S. has chosen not to ratify Additional Protocol II though it considers the majority of the treaty's provisions to reflect binding customary international law.

[19] See, for example, Amnesty International, "Yemen/USA: government must not sanction extra-judicial executions," press release, November 8, 2002, http://www.amnesty.org/ar/library/asset/AMR51/168/2002/ar/ac72c772-fae9-11dd-8917-49d72d0853f5/amr511682002en.pdf (accessed March 10, 2012). Human rights law is beyond the scope of this paper.

[20] See, for example, U.S. Congress, House of Representatives, Rise of the Drones II: Examining the Legality of Unmanned Targeting: Hearings before the Subcommittee on National Security and Foreign Affairs of the Committee on Oversight and Government Reform, 111th Cong., 2nd sess., 2010, 18-25 (statement of Professor Mary Ellen O'Connell), http://www.fas.org/irp/congress/2010_hr/drones2.pdf (accessed January 21, 2012).

[21] See, for example, Mary Ellen O'Connell, "Unlawful Killing with Combat Drones: A Case Study of Pakistan, 2004-2009," Notre Dame Law School Legal Studies Research Paper No. 09-43, http://ssrn.com/abstract=1501144 (accessed January 20, 2012).

[22] See, for example, Gordon Lubold, "Anwar al-Awlaki: Is it legal to kill an American in war on terror?," *Christian Science Monitor*, April 8, 2010.

[23] Complaint for Declaratory and Injunctive Relief at 11, Al-Aulaqi v. Obama, 727 F. Supp. 2d 1 (D.D.C. 2010) (No. 1:10-cv-01469).

[24] Al-Aulaqi v. Obama, 727 F. Supp. 2d 1, 8-9 (D.D.C. 2010). Judge Bates, the presiding judge, dismissed the case on the grounds that Nasser al-Awlaki's father lacked standing to assert his son's interests, and that the case involved a non-justiciable political question.

[25] Peter Finn, "Secret U.S. memo sanctioned killing of Aulaqi," *Washington Post*, September 30, 2011. The Justice Department's Office of Legal Counsel has been characterized as "the most important government office you've never heard of. . . . . Its carefully worded opinions are regarded as binding precedent--final say on what the president and all his agencies can and cannot legally do." Daniel Klaidman, Evan Thomas, and Stuart Taylor Jr., "Palace Revolt," *Newsweek*, February 6, 2006, 34.

[26] Charlie Savage, "Secret U.S. Memo Made Legal Case to Kill a Citizen," *New York Times*, October 8, 2011.

[27] Ibid.

[28] Ibid.

[29] J. David Goodman, "Awlaki Killing Incites Criticism on Left and Libertarian Right," *The Lede*, entry posted September 30, 2011, http://thelede.blogs.nytimes.com/2011/09/30/awlaki-killing-sparks-criticism-on-left-and-libertarian-right/ (accessed March 10, 2012). For an example of criticism from the left, see Glenn Greenwald, "The due-process-free assassination of U.S. citizens is now reality," September 30, 2011, http://www.salon.com/2011/09/30/awlaki_6/singleton/ (accessed October 20, 2011). For an example of criticism from the right, see Martin Gould and Ashley Martella, "Napolitano: Obama 'Shredding the Constitution,'" October 23, 2011, http://www.newsmax.com/Headline/Napolitano-Obama-Impeached-Awlaki/2011/10/22/id/415400 (accessed March 10, 2012).

[30] See, for example, Peter Finn, "Political, legal experts want release of Justice Dept. memo supporting killing of Anwar al-Awlaki," *Washington Post*, October 7, 2011. See also Editorial, "The Power to Kill," *New York Times*, March 10, 2012. The government still refuses to even acknowledge the OLC opinion's existence.

[31] Jeh Charles Johnson, "National security law, lawyers and lawyering in the Obama Administration," speech, Yale Law School, February 22, 2012, http://www.cfr.org/national-security-and-defense/jeh-johnsons-speech-national-security-law-lawyers-lawyering-obama-administration/p27448 (accessed March 5, 2012) (hereinafter Johnson speech). U.S. Department of Justice, "Attorney General Eric Holder Speaks at Northwestern University School of Law," March 5, 2012, http://www.justice.gov/iso/opa/ag/speeches/2012/ag-speech-1203051.html (accessed March 6, 2012) (hereinafter Holder speech).

[32] See, for example, Andrew Cohen, "On 'Targeted Killing' Speech, Eric Holder Strikes Out," *theatlantic.com*, entry posted March 6, 2012, http://www.theatlantic.com/national/archive/2012/03/on-targeted-killing-speech-eric-holder-strikes-out/254000/ (accessed March 17, 2012).

[33] The law of war principles are necessity, distinction, proportionality, and humanity (also referred to as unnecessary suffering). Holder defined these principles as follows:

> The principle of necessity requires that the target have definite military value. The principle of distinction requires that only lawful targets - such as combatants, civilians directly participating in hostilities, and military objectives - may be targeted intentionally. Under the principle of proportionality, the anticipated collateral damage must not be excessive in relation to the anticipated military

advantage. Finally, the principle of humanity requires us to use weapons that will not inflict unnecessary suffering.

Holder speech. Holder briefly discussed the concept of "imminent threat," advocating that in the case of potential terrorist acts imminence must be evaluated based on the "relevant window of opportunity to act" rather than in a temporal sense. As to the feasibility of capture, he provided no specifics, stating merely that, "Whether the capture of a U.S. citizen terrorist is feasible is a fact-specific, and potentially time-sensitive, question." Ibid.

[34] Ibid.

[35] Ibid.

[36] Ibid.

[37] Ibid.

[38] In a speech to the American Society of International Law, Koh addressed the Obama Administration's view of the use of force and U.S. targeting practices. He justified the use of force, and targeted killing by implication, within the contexts of both armed conflict and self-defense:

> [A]s a matter of international law, the United States is in an armed conflict with al-Qaeda, as well as the Taliban and associated forces, in response to the horrific 9/11 attacks, and may use force consistent with its inherent right to self-defense under international law. . . . [I]n this ongoing armed conflict, the United States has the authority under international law, and the responsibility to its citizens, to use force, including lethal force, to defend itself, including by targeting persons such as high level al-Qaeda leaders who are planning attacks.

Harold Hongju Koh, "The Obama Administration and International Law," speech, Annual Meeting of the American Society of International Law, Washington, DC, March 25, 2010, http://www.state.gov/s/l/releases/remarks/139119.htm (accessed December 15, 2011); John O. Brennan, "Strengthening our Security by Adhering to our Values and Laws," speech, Program on Law and Security, Harvard Law School, Cambridge, MA, September 16, 2011, http://www.whitehouse.gov/the-press-office/2011/09/16/remarks-john-o-brennan-strengthening-our-security-adhering-our-values-an (accessed January 20, 2012) (hereinafter Brennan speech).

[39] Nils Melzer, *Interpretive Guidance on the Notion of Direct Participation in Hostilities Under International Humanitarian Law* (Geneva: International Committee of the Red Cross, 2009), 70.

[40] Ibid., 34.

[41] See, for example, Kenneth Watkin, "Opportunity Lost: Organized Armed Groups and the ICRC 'Direct Participation in Hostilities' Interpretive Guidance," *New York University Journal of International Law and Politics* 42, no. 3 (2010): 641.

[42] See, for example, U.S. Congress, statement of Professor Mary Ellen O'Connell.

[43] Charlie Savage, "At White House, Weighing Limits of Terror Fight," *New York Times*, September 15, 2011. According to Savage, lawyers in the State and Defense Departments disagree on the legal authority of the U.S. to target terrorists outside Afghanistan and portions of Pakistan.

[44] In his speech, Holder asserted that,

> Our legal authority is not limited to the battlefields in Afghanistan. Indeed, neither Congress nor our federal courts has limited the geographic scope of our ability to use force to the current conflict in Afghanistan. We are at war with a stateless enemy, prone to shifting operations from country to country. Over the last three years alone, al Qaeda and its associates have directed several attacks – fortunately, unsuccessful – against us from countries other than Afghanistan. Our government has both a responsibility and a right to protect this nation and its people from such threats.

Holder speech. John Brennan likewise has stated that, "The U.S. does not view our authority to use military force against al-Qa'ida as being restricted solely to 'hot' battlefields like Afghanistan." Brennan speech. Moreover, in the detainee case *Hamdan v. Rumsfeld*, the U.S. Supreme Court found that the United States is engaged in a non-international armed conflict with Al Qaeda. Hamdan v. Rumsfeld, 548 U.S. 557, 630 (2006).

[45] UN Charter, art. 51 provides that, "Nothing in the present Charter shall impair the inherent right of individual or collective self-defence if an armed attack occurs against a Member of the United Nations . . . ." Indeed, in response to the September 11 attacks, the UN Security Council unanimously passed two resolutions in short order, both reaffirming the inherent right of individual and collective self-defense. See UN Security Council, Resolution 1368 (September 12, 2001), http://www.un.org/News/Press/docs/2001/SC7143.doc.htm (accessed November 15, 2011). See also UN Security Council, Resolution 1373 (September 28, 2001), http://www.un.org/News/Press/docs/2001/sc7158.doc.htm (accessed November 15, 2011).

[46] W. Hays Parks, "Memorandum of Law: Executive Order 12333 and Assassination," *The Army Lawyer* (December 1989): 7.

[47] As DoD General Counsel Johnson observed, "over the last 10 years al Qaeda has not only become more decentralized, it has also, for the most part, migrated away from Afghanistan to other places where it can find safe haven." Johnson speech.

[48] UN Charter, art. 2(4).

[49] Holder speech.

[50] With respect to Yemen, see, for example, Priest, "U.S. military teams, intelligence." Pakistan has reportedly denied some requests to conduct UAS strikes, indicating that the U.S. has been unable to simply impose its will on other states. Karen DeYoung, "Secrecy defines Obama's drone war," *Washington Post*, December 19, 2011 According to DeYoung, after agreeing in 2004 to U.S. targeting of "al-Qaeda and Taliban sanctuaries in Pakistan" that "were within the limits of geographic 'boxes' in the tribal regions" bordering Afghanistan, "[b]y mid-2008, Musharraf had turned down nearly as many strikes as he had approved." Ibid.

[51] Parks, "Memorandum of Law," 7. Parks cites, for example, an 1804-1805 Marine expedition to Libya to kill or capture Barbary pirates and General Pershing's 1916 Mexican campaign to kill or capture Pancho Villa. Ibid. For a broader discussion of the exercise of self-defense when a state is unwilling or unable to suppress a threat coming from within its borders, see Michael D. Banks, "Addressing State (Ir-)Responsibility: The Use of Military Force as Self-Defense in International Counter-Terrorism Operations," *Military Law Review* 200 (Summer 2009): 54.

[52] George W. Bush, Address to a Joint Session of Congress and the American People, Washington, DC, September 20, 2001, http://georgewbush-whitehouse.archives.gov/news/releases/2001/09/20010920-8.html (accessed December 16, 2011).

[53] Priest, "U.S. military teams, intelligence." See also Shane, "U.S. Approves Targeted Killing." While considered an unprecedented move, the Bush Administration had reportedly earlier given the CIA limited authority to kill U.S. citizens affiliated with terrorist organizations. Priest, "U.S. military teams, intelligence."

[54] Unclassified Declaration in Support of Formal Claim of State Secrets Privilege by James R. Clapper, Director of National Intelligence, Al-Aulaqi v. Obama, 727 F. Supp. 2d 1 (D.D.C. 2010) (No. 1:10-cv-01469).

[55] U.S. Constitution, Amendment 5.

[56] The ACLU and CCR, for example asserted that,

> Defendants' policy of targeted killings violates the Fifth Amendment by authorizing, outside of armed conflict, the killing of U.S. citizens . . . without due process of law in circumstances in which they do not present concrete, specific, and imminent threats to life or physical safety, and where there are means other than lethal force that could reasonably be employed to neutralize any such threat.

Complaint for Declaratory and Injunctive Relief at 10, Al-Aulaqi v. Obama. Democratic Congressman Dennis Kucinich characterized al-Awlaki's killing as a "dangerous legal precedent [that] allows the government to target U.S. citizens abroad for being suspected of involvement in terrorism, in subversion of their most basic constitutional rights and due process of law." "Kucinich on the Extrajudicial Killing on Anwar al-Awlaki: Wrong Legally, Constitutionally and Morally," September 30, 2011, *Congressman Dennis J. Kucinich*, http://kucinich.house.gov/News/DocumentSingle.aspx?DocumentID=262506 (accessed January 15, 2012). Moreover, in a statement confirming al-Awlaki's death AQAP wrote, "The Americans killed the scholar Shaykh Anwar al-Awlaki and Samir Khan, but they did not prove any crime they committed and they never presented any proof against them from their laws of unjust freedom." Mackenzie Weinger, "Al Qaeda: Al-Awlaki killing unlawful," Politico, October 10, 2011, http://www.politico.com/news/stories/1011/65546.html#ixzz1n3k2TeRq (accessed November 15, 2011).

[57] Complaint for Declaratory and Injunctive Relief at 10, Al-Aulaqi v. Obama. The circumstances the ACLU and CCR asserted might justify targeted killing outside of armed

conflict include the targeted individual presenting, "concrete, specific, and imminent threats to life or physical safety." Ibid.

[58] Andrew Kent, "The Constitution and the Laws of War During the Civil War," *Notre Dame Law Review* 85, no. 5 (2010): 1851.

[59] Ibid., 1872-1880.

[60] The Prize Cases, 67 U.S. 635, 672 (1862).

[61] Ibid.

[62] Ibid., 673.

[63] Ibid., 674.

[64] Ex Parte Quirin, 317 U.S. 1 (1942).

[65] Ibid., 37.

[66] Hamdi v. Rumsfeld, 524 U.S. 507, 519 (2004), citing Brief for Respondents, 3.

[67] Ibid., 510.

[68] Mathews v. Eldridge, 424 U.S. 319 (1976).

[69] Hamdi v. Rumsfeld, 533.

[70] Ibid., 534.

[71] Robert J. Delahunty and Christopher J. Motz, "Killing al-Awlaki: The Domestic Legal Issues," *University of St. Thomas School of Law Legal Studies Research Paper No. 11-38*, 36, http://papers.ssrn.com/abstract=1963976 (accessed February 5, 2012).

[72] Richard Murphy and John Radsan, "Due Process and Targeted Killing of Terrorists," *Cardozo Law Review* 31, no. 2 (2009): 405, 437-445. Murphy and Radsan, who concede that the likelihood of such review would be rare, suggest as a possibility a proceeding in which "the plaintiff—who might be a survivor of an attempted targeted killing or an appropriate next friend—claims that the attack was unconstitutional either because it violated the Fifth Amendment on a 'shock the conscience' theory or because it constituted excessive force under the Fourth amendment." Ibid., 440.

[73] Holder speech.

[74] See, for example, Feisal G. Mohamed, "The Assassination President?," July 19, 2011, http://www.huffingtonpost.com/feisal-g-mohamed/obama-drones_b_899885.html (accessed January 22, 2012). The assassination ban is contained in Executive Order no. 12333, United States Intelligence Activities, *Code of Federal Regulations* title 3, sec. 200 (1982).

[75] Elizabeth B. Bazan, *Assassination Ban and E.O. 12333: A Brief Summary*, (Washington, DC: U.S. Library of Congress, Congressional Research Service, January 4, 2002), 1-2.

[76] Parks, "Memorandum of Law," 4.

[77] Ibid.

[78] "Members of the armed forces of a Party to a conflict . . . are combatants, that is to say, they have the right to participate directly in hostilities." Additional Protocol I, art. 43(2).

[79] See, for example, Cullen, "The Role of Targeted Killing," 25. See also Gary Solis, "CIA drone attacks produce America's own unlawful combatants," *Washington Post*, March 10, 2010.

[80] DeYoung, "Secrecy defines Obama's drone war."

[81] *Foreign Murder of United States Nationals*, U.S. Code, title 18, sec. 1119.

[82] See, for example, Philip Dore, "Greenlighting American Citizens: Proceed with Caution," *Louisiana Law Review* 72, no. 1 (2011): 255. See also Kevin Jon Heller, "Let's Call Killing al-Awlaki what it is—Murder," April 8, 2010, http://opiniojuris.org/2010/04/08/lets-call-killing-al-awlaki-what-it-is-murder/ (accessed January 22, 2012).

[83] Murray v. Schooner Charming Betsy, 6 U.S. 64 (1804).

[84] But see Dore, "Greenlighting American Citizens," 255.

[85] Heller, "Let's Call Killing al-Awlaki what it is—Murder."

[86] *Foreign Murder of United States Nationals*, § 1119(c)(1).

[87] This issue arose with respect to the use of certain interrogation techniques, including waterboarding, by CIA personnel in reliance on Justice Department opinions issued during the Bush Administration that were later revoked. Many urged President Bush to pardon the CIA personnel involved before leaving office, but he declined to do so. Although Attorney General Holder characterized waterboarding as illegal torture, President Obama announced that CIA personnel acting in reliance on legal advice from the Justice Department would not be prosecuted. Mark Mazzetti and Scott Shane, "Interrogation Memos Detail Harsh Tactics by the C.I.A.," *New York Times*, April 16, 2009.

[88] Barack H. Obama, "Remarks to White House Senior Staff," January 21, 2009, http://www.gpoaccess.gov/presdocs/2009/DCPD200900012.htm (accessed December 10, 2011). Moreover, President Obama issued a memorandum on transparency and open government as one of his first acts upon taking office. Barack H. Obama, Memorandum, "Transparency and Open Government," *Federal Register* 74, no. 15 (January 26, 2009): 4685.

[89] "Your Interview with the President – 2012," January 30, 2012, *YouTube*, video file, http://www.youtube.com/watch?v=eeTj5qMGTAI (accessed February 15, 2012). Panetta, interview by Scott Pelley.

[90] Susan Viscuso, Central Intelligence Agency, letter to Nathan Freed Wessler, American Civil Liberties Union, November 17, 2011, http://www.aclu.org/national-security/central-intelligence-agency-response-al-awlaki-foia-request (accessed January 11, 2012). Paul B. Colborn, U.S. Department of Justice Office of Legal Counsel, letter to Nathan Freed Wessler,

American Civil Liberties Union, November 14, 2011, http://www.aclu.org/files/assets/aclu_administrative_appeal_of_olc_refusal_to_confirm_or_deny_existence_of_responsive_records.pdf (accessed January 11, 2012).

[91] Complaint, New York Times Company v. Department of Justice (S.D.N.Y. 2011) (No. 11-CIV-9336).

[92] Benjamin Wittes, "Kenneth Anderson on Charlie Savage's Story and Secrecy," *Lawfare*, entry posted October 9, 2011, http://www.lawfareblog.com/2011/10/kenneth-anderson-on-charlie-savages-story-and-secrecy/ (accessed December 5, 2011). This partly reflects the growing contemporary paradox of "information that is public but classified." Scott Shane, "A Closed-Mouth Policy Even on Open Secrets," *New York Times*, October 4, 2011.

[93] See, for example, Mary Ellen O'Connell, "Killing Awlaki was illegal, immoral and dangerous," *Global Public Square*, entry posted October 1, 2011, http://globalpublicsquare.blogs.cnn.com/2011/10/01/killing-awlaki-was-illegal-immoral-and-dangerous/ (accessed March 12, 2012).

[94] See, for example, Peter Catapano, "Views to a Kill," *Opinionator: The Thread*, entry posted October 14, 2011, http://opinionator.blogs.nytimes.com/2011/10/14/views-to-a-kill/ (accessed March 12, 2012). Recall, however, that some 65 percent of Americans appear to approve of the targeted killing of suspected terrorists who are U.S. citizens. *Washington Post*, "Washington Post-ABC News Poll."

[95] Jack Goldsmith, "Release the al-Aulaqi OLC opinion, Or Its Reasoning," *Lawfare*, entry posted October 3, 2011, http://www.lawfareblog.com/2011/10/release-the-al-aulaqi-olc-opinion-or-its-reasoning/ (accessed March 11, 2012).

[96] Ibid.

[97] Panetta, interview by Scott Pelley.

[98] Holder speech.

[99] Ibid.

[100] Charlie Savage, "A Not-Quite Confirmation of a Memo Approving Killing," *New York Times*, March 8, 2012. Senator Ron Wyden also rebuked the administration "for not providing Congress with the legal basis for the killing of the U.S. citizen." Ellen Nakashima, "Democrat balks over secrecy on Awlaki killing," *Washington Post*, February 18, 2012.

[101] The Public Committee Against Torture v. Israel, HCJ 769/02, para. 40.

[102] See, for example, Murphy and Radsan, "Due Process and Targeted Killing of Terrorists," 446-449. "Created in 1989, the statutory Inspector General (IG) is responsible for independent oversight of the CIA. The IG is nominated by the president and confirmed by the Senate, and may only be removed from office by the president." Central Intelligence Agency, "Inspector General," *Offices of CIA*, https://www.cia.gov/offices-of-cia/inspector-general/index.html (accessed March 10, 2012).

[103] See, for example, "Judicial Scrutiny Before Death," editorial, *New York Times*, December 12, 2010.

[104] Holder speech.

[105] Murphy and Radsan, "Due Process and Targeted Killing of Terrorists," 447.

[106] According to DoD's latest strategic guidance, "For the foreseeable future, *the United States will continue to take an active approach to countering [violent extremists]* by . . . directly striking the most dangerous groups and individuals when necessary." Leon E. Panetta, *Sustaining Global Leadership: Priorities for 21st Century Defense* (Washington, DC: U.S. Department of Defense, January 2012), 1.

www.ingramcontent.com/pod-product-compliance
Lightning Source LLC
Chambersburg PA
CBHW081807280526
45789CB00008B/3031